The *Blue Plate Diner* Cookbook

The *Blue Plate Diner*
Cookbook

Tim Lloyd & James Novak

With Bakery Recipes by Sara Whalen

Itchy Cat Press
Blue Mounds, Wisconsin

Second edition, first printing
Copyright © 1999 by Tim Lloyd and James Novak

Itchy Cat Press
A Division of Flying Fish Graphics
5452 Highway K
Blue Mounds, Wisconsin 53517

Designed by Flying Fish Graphics, Blue Mounds, Wisconsin
Photographs by Brent Nicastro
Printed in Korea
Permission to use clip art granted by Art Direction Book Company, Inc.

Library of Congress Control Number: 2005934007

ISBN 0-9761450-2-2

Introduction

The Blue Plate Diner is a part of the Atwood neighborhood. It's not just *in* the neighborhood, it's *part* of it. And I think that's an important distinction.

The Atwood neighborhood is one of the oldest in Madison. It was a lively place, mostly a blue-collar area, when the veterans returned to wives, sweethearts, friends, and family after World War II. For many years, this building was Severson's Gas Station, later owned by the Havey brothers.

Atwood lost much of its vibrancy in later years, perhaps culminating in the 1970s when the Eastwood Theater was reduced to showing X-rated films. Many storefronts were vacant, buildings were running down, and neighborhood spirit was at a low ebb.

Now the Atwood neighborhood is in the midst of a vital renaissance. New shops and restaurants, new young families, spruced-up and renovated buildings, streetside plantings, the Barrymore Theatre, and more. I like to think that the Blue Plate Diner has played a part in this renaissance, and will continue to do so, as the neighborhood continues to reinvent itself in the new millennium.

When we went to remodel the old gas station into a restaurant, we went to architect Ed Linville, who immediately sensed the possibilities. With us,

BEST YOU EVER ATE

CHILI

he wanted to recapture that postwar feeling by designing a "late 40s-style" diner—not one that looked like a stage set, but an honest diner that could serve good, wholesome, comforting food, a place where everybody would feel welcome—young and old, blue collars and business suits, students and retirees. I had fun offering my personal toaster and blender to be turned into neon art, and donating my Fiesta Ware collection. Everything customers see around them in the diner today, in blue and silver and neon, is the result of our efforts, as expressed in Ed's creative design.

What makes the diner really tick, however, is not the design, not even the food (although both have received their share of praise) but the *people*. I have been most fortunate to attract and keep together a terrific staff, which in turn has managed to attract an equally great group of regular customers. Even people who visit for the first time say they feel instantly at home in the diner. I like to think that their mood changes as soon as they walk through the door. Together, staff and customers have created what I dreamed of from the very beginning—a true neighborhood diner where everything and everyone feels comfortable.

Welcome to the Blue Plate Diner.

—Monty Schiro

Special thanks to
Brian "Little Deb" Boehm
Gerrard "G" Meurer
Steven "Mr. Clean" Hoyle

Cooking is not an exact science. It's an art. Use these recipes as a guide. Add and delete ingredients to suit your own tastes.

Have fun,
Tim

Soups & Salads

Soups & Salads

*S*oup is good food. You can open a can and have a quick, easy meal or you can take just a little effort and try these simple recipes. In the process of making soup, you will fill your home with fantastic aromas. You will be using mostly fresh ingredients, eliminating most chemicals and preservatives. Making soup at home is fun, easy, and inexpensive.

Making soup is not an exact science. Each of our tastes differs, and we might change the quantities of ingredients or even eliminate some of them. In our soup recipes we do not designate the quantities of pepper or salt; use your good judgment to suit your personal taste and needs. If you prefer, use heavy cream, half-and-half, or 2% milk instead of whole milk. If you don't like garlic, don't use it. Soup is a comfort food. Make yourself comfortable!

Tim Lloyd has been making soup for more than 20 years and since 1990 at Monty's Blue Plate Diner. When he looks into a refrigerator, he sees the potential of almost every ingredient in sight for making a nutritious pot of soup. Tim's soup recipes are like magic. They follow a similar pattern and thus after you've made a few of them, you'll soon be able to make many more just by repeating the general pattern you have learned to follow in past recipes.

Tim starts with a basic mirepoix, a mixture of vegetables used to flavor the recipe. The aromatic vegetables are diced and then sautéed in olive

1

oil to bring out their flavors at the beginning of soup-making. In an easy second step, most of the other ingredients are added to the pot, brought to a boil, and then simmered. Fragile ingredients such as pasta, or those that might burn easily to the bottom of the pan such as sour cream, roux, milk, or cheese, are added near the end of the process. Most recipes will make approximately 4 quarts and serve 6-8 guests.

Most restaurants and chefs use soup bases when making soups. Soup bases obviate the very lengthy process of boiling meats or vegetables to obtain a richly flavored concentrate. Many of the Blue Plate Diner soup recipes call for chicken, beef, mushroom, or vegetable soup bases. These are readily available at most major supermarkets. Soup bases come in various qualities. Buy the best. A good-quality base will look like paste, not powder. On the label of a good soup base, the first ingredient listed will be the item after which the base is named, e.g. beef, chicken, mushroom. In poorer quality soup bases the number one ingredient will be salt. If you use a lower-quality soup base where the primary ingredient is salt, you will have to be careful to taste the soup before adding "salt to taste."

A roux is used to thicken many soups. Here is Tim's basic roux recipe, which will be required often in the recipes that follow.

Roux

Ingredients:
1/2 lb. margarine
1 1/2 cups white flour

Instructions:
Melt margarine in a pan on low heat. Gradually stir in flour with whisk or a wooden spoon. Cook 15 minutes on low heat while occasionally stirring briskly. Add a little roux at a time, until you are satisfied with the consistency of the soup or sauce. Remember that warm roux mixes better than cold roux, and that you should always cook any soup or sauce for at least 15 minutes after adding roux, to eliminate any "pasty" flavor.

Yield: 1 1/2 cups.

Pumpkin Soup

Ingredients:
1 small onion, diced
4 stalks celery, diced
2 tb. olive oil
1-28 oz. can pumpkin (not spiced)
6 cups water
1 tb. salt
1/2 c. sugar
1 tb. cinnamon
2 cups milk

Instructions:
In a 6-quart pot sauté the onion and celery in the olive oil for 10 minutes on medium heat until tender. Add all other ingredients except milk. Bring to a boil, then simmer for one hour. Stir in milk and simmer for an additional 10 minutes.

Yield: Approximately 3 quarts; serves 6-8.

Potato Leek Soup

Ingredients:

1 medium onion, diced
3 leeks, medium cut
3 celery stalks, diced
2 tbs. olive oil
3 large potatoes, peeled and diced
3 quarts water
salt to taste
white pepper to taste
1 tb. dried parsley
3 dashes Tabasco sauce
1 tb. chives
1 tb. vegetable base
1 1/2 cup roux (page 2)
1 cup sour cream

Instructions:

In a 6-quart pot sauté the onions, leeks, and celery in olive oil for 10 minutes on medium heat until tender. Add all other ingredients except roux and sour cream. Bring to a boil and then simmer 45 minutes. Add roux and stir until thoroughly blended. Simmer 15 minutes until soup thickens. Add sour cream and stir until blended. Simmer an additional 5 minutes.

Yield 4 quarts; serves 6-8.

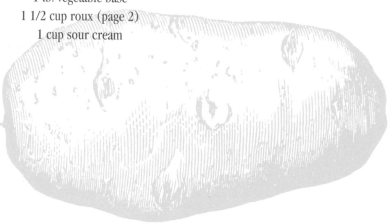

Sweet & Sour Cabbage Soup

Ingredients:

3 stalks celery, diced
4 medium carrots, sliced
1 tb. crushed garlic
1 medium onion, diced
2 tbs. olive oil
2 large potatoes, diced
1/2 head cabbage, chopped
1-28 oz. can diced tomatoes
3 quarts water
1 cup honey
1 cup cider vinegar
1 tb. vegetable base
salt to taste
black pepper to taste

Instructions:

In a 6-quart pot, sauté celery, carrots, garlic, and onions in olive oil for 10 minutes on medium heat until tender. Add all other ingredients and bring to a boil. Simmer on low heat for one hour.

Yield: 4 quarts; serves 6-8.

Mushroom Barley Soup

Ingredients:

3 stalks celery, diced
4 medium carrots, sliced
1 medium onion, diced
2 tbs. olive oil
2 lbs. mushrooms, sliced
1 cup med. pearl barley (not instant)
3 quarts water
salt to taste
pepper to taste
1 tb. vegetable or mushroom base
1 tb. parsley

Instructions:

In a 6-quart pot, sauté celery, carrots, and onions in olive oil for 10 minutes on medium heat until tender. Add all other ingredients and bring to a boil. Simmer on low heat for one hour.

Yield: 4 quarts; serves 6-8.

Spicy Peanut Soup

Ingredients:

2 medium carrots, sliced
1 medium onion, diced
3 stalks celery, diced
2 tbs. olive oil
1 cup med. pearl barley (not instant)
2 cups peanut butter
3 quarts water
1 tb. red pepper flakes
1 finely chopped jalapeno pepper
2 tbs. honey
salt to taste
black pepper to taste
Tabasco sauce to taste

Instructions:

In a 6-quart pot, sauté the carrots, onion, and celery in olive oil on medium heat until tender. Add all other ingredients. Bring to a boil and simmer for one hour.

Yield: 4 quarts; serves 6-8.

Tomato Parmesan Soup

Ingredients:

1 medium onion, diced
4 medium carrots, sliced
1 tb. crushed garlic
3 stalks celery, diced
2 tbs. olive oil
3 quarts water
1-28 oz. can of diced tomatoes
Tabasco sauce to taste
salt to taste
black pepper to taste
1 1/2 cup roux (page 2)
1 lb. shredded Cheddar cheese
8 oz. shredded Parmesan cheese
3 cups penne or elbow noodles

Instructions:

In a 6-quart pot, sauté the onion, carrots, garlic, and celery in the olive oil on medium heat for 10 minutes until tender. Add other ingredients except roux, pasta, and cheeses. Bring to a boil. Simmer for 45 minutes on low heat. Add roux and stir until thoroughly blended. Slowly add cheeses while continuously stirring until they are blended into the soup. Cook and add pasta. Simmer another 5 minutes on very low heat.

Yield: 4 quarts; serves 6-8.

Cream of Mushroom Soup

Ingredients:

1 medium onion, diced
3 stalks celery, diced
2 lbs. mushrooms, sliced
1 tb. garlic
2 tbs. olive oil
1/4 cup soy sauce
3 quarts water
2 tbs. dried basil
2 tbs. mushroom base
salt to taste
black pepper to taste
Tabasco sauce to taste
1 1/2 cup roux (page 2)
2 cups milk
1 cup sour cream

Instructions:

In a 6-quart pot, sauté onion, celery, mushrooms, and garlic in olive oil for 10 minutes on medium heat until tender. Add all other ingredients except roux, milk, and sour cream. Bring to a boil and simmer for 45 minutes. Add roux and stir until blended. Simmer 15 minutes until the soup thickens. Add milk and sour cream, and stir until blended. Simmer an additional 5 minutes.

Yield: 4 quarts; serves 6-8.

Reuben Soup

Ingredients:
4 medium carrots, sliced
1 medium onion, diced
1 tb. crushed garlic
3 stalks celery, diced
2 tbs. olive oil
2 large potatoes, diced
1 pound cooked corned beef, diced
or shredded
1 lb. sauerkraut, drained
3 quarts water
2 tbs. Dijon mustard
1 1/2 oz. red balsamic vinegar
2 tbs. beef base

Instructions:
In a 6-quart pot, sauté the carrots, onion, garlic, and celery in olive oil on medium heat until tender. Add all other ingredients. Bring to a boil and simmer for one hour.

Yield: 4 quarts; serves 6-8.

Navy Bean Soup

Ingredients:

2 stalks celery, diced
1 medium onion, diced
4 medium carrots, sliced
2 tbs. olive oil
4 cups dry navy beans
2 cups diced ham (add ham bone
if available)
3 quarts water
salt to taste (use caution—ham
already has a high salt content)
pepper to taste
2 tbs. molasses
2 tbs. Dijon mustard
2 tbs. ketchup

Instructions:

In a 6-quart pot sauté the celery, onion, and carrots in olive oil on medium heat for 10 minutes until tender. Add all other ingredients and bring to a boil. Simmer covered for 2 hours until beans are tender.

Yield: 4 quarts; serves 6-8.

Veggie Lentil Soup

Ingredients:

1 medium onion, diced
4 medium carrots, sliced
3 stalks celery, diced
2 tbs. olive oil
1 lb. mushrooms, sliced
1-14 1/2 oz. can diced tomatoes
2 med. potatoes, diced
3 cups lentils
4 quarts water
salt to taste
pepper to taste
1 tb. vegetable base
4 dashes Tabasco sauce

Instructions:

In a 6-quart pot, sauté the onion, carrots, and celery in the olive oil on medium heat for 10 minutes until tender. Add all other ingredients. Bring to a boil. Simmer for one hour on low heat.

Yield: 4 quarts; serves 6-8.

Chicken Mushroom Soup

Ingredients:

4 medium carrots, sliced
1 medium onion, diced
4 stalks celery, diced
1 tb. crushed garlic
2 tbs. olive oil
2 lbs. mushrooms, sliced
1 lb. chicken breast, diced
3 quarts water
1 cup cream
salt to taste
pepper to taste
1 tb. crushed sage
1 tb. parsley
1 1/2 tbs. mushroom base
1 1/2 tbs. chicken base
1 1/2 cups roux (page 2)

Instructions:

In a 6-quart pot, sauté carrots, onion, celery, and garlic in olive oil on medium heat for 10 minutes until tender. Add all other ingredients except roux and bring to a boil. Cover pot and simmer on low heat for 45 minutes. Add roux and stir until thoroughly blended. Simmer 15 minutes until soup thickens.

Yield: 4 quarts; serves 6-8.

This soup is delicious!

Cauliflower Cheese Soup

Ingredients:

1 medium onion, diced
4 medium carrots, sliced
1 tb. crushed garlic
3 stalks celery, diced
2 tbs. olive oil
3 quarts water
1 medium head cauliflower, broken into florets
salt to taste
black pepper to taste
1 cup roux (page 2)
1 lb. shredded Cheddar cheese
8 oz. shredded Parmesan cheese
2 cups milk

Instructions:

In a 6-quart pot, sauté the onion, carrots, garlic, and celery in the olive oil on medium heat for 10 minutes until tender. Add all other ingredients except the roux, milk, and cheeses. Bring to a boil. Simmer for one hour on low heat. Add roux and stir until thoroughly blended. Slowly add cheeses while stirring continuously until they are blended into the soup. Add milk while stirring. Simmer another 20 minutes on very low heat, stirring every five minutes .

Yield: 4 quarts; serves 6-8.

Ham, Cheese, & Beer Soup

Ingredients:
1 medium onion, diced
3 stalks celery, diced
1 tb. crushed garlic
2 tbs. olive oil
3 quarts water
1 tb. beef base
1 tb. chicken base
1 lb. diced ham
12 oz. beer
1 cup roux (page 2)
3 cups shredded Cheddar cheese

Instructions:
In a 6-quart pot, sauté onion, celery, and garlic in olive oil on medium heat for 10 minutes until tender. Add all other ingredients except roux and cheese and bring to a boil. Cover pot and simmer on low heat for 45 minutes. Add roux and stir until thoroughly blended. Simmer 15 minutes until soup thickens. Slowly add cheese, stirring continuously until cheese blends into the broth.

Yield: 4 quarts; serves 6-8.

Split Pea & Ham Soup

Ingredients:

1 tb. crushed garlic
4 medium carrots, sliced
3 stalks celery, diced
1 medium onion, diced
2 tbs. olive oil
4 quarts water
4 cups dried split peas
1 lb. diced ham (add ham bone
if available)
2 tbs. ham base
2 tb. chicken base
salt to taste
black pepper to taste

Instructions:

In a 6-quart pot, sauté the garlic, carrots, celery, and onion in olive oil for 10 minutes on medium heat until tender. Add all other ingredients. Bring to a boil and simmer for one and a quarter hours.

Yield: 4 quarts; serves 6-8.

Greek Spinach Soup

Ingredients:

2 10-oz. packages of frozen
chopped spinach
1 medium onion, diced
3 stalks celery, diced
1 tb. crushed garlic
2 tbs. olive oil
1 lb. mushrooms, sliced
2 large potatoes, diced
1 tb. oregano
3 quarts water
salt to taste
black pepper to taste
8 oz. crumbled Feta cheese

Instructions:

Defrost spinach. In a 6-quart pot, sauté onion, celery, and garlic in olive oil on medium heat for 10 minutes until tender. Add all other ingredients except Feta cheese and bring to a boil. Cover pot and simmer on low heat for 45 minutes. Slowly add crumbled Feta cheese, stirring continuously until cheese blends into the broth.

Yield: 4 quarts; serves 6-8.

Scottish Vegetable Soup

Ingredients:

4 medium carrots, sliced
1 medium onion, diced
2 celery stalks, diced
2 tbs. olive oil
2 large potatoes, peeled and diced
1 lb. mushrooms, sliced
1 46-oz. can tomato juice
salt to taste
pepper to taste
2 tbs. parsley
2 tbs. vegetable base
3 cups oatmeal (quick oats)

Instructions:

In a 6-quart pot, sauté the carrots, onion, and celery in the olive oil on medium heat for 10 minutes until tender. Add all other ingredients except oatmeal and bring to a boil. Cover pot and simmer for 45 minutes. Add oatmeal and stir into mixture. Simmer for an additional 15 minutes.

Yield: 4 quarts; serves 6-8.

Makes me feel strong!

Tomato Dill Soup

Ingredients:

1 medium onion, diced
2 celery stalks, diced
1 tb. crushed garlic
2 tbs. olive oil
1 28-oz. can crushed tomatoes
4 tbs. dried dill weed
1/2 cup honey
2 quarts water
salt to taste
pepper to taste
2 cups whole milk

Instructions:

In a 6-quart pot, sauté the onion, celery, and garlic in the olive oil on medium heat for 10 minutes until tender. Add all the other ingredients except the milk and bring to a boil. Simmer for 45 minutes. Stir in milk and simmer another 15 minutes, stirring occasionally.

Yield: 3 quarts; serves 6-8.

Chinese Vegetable Soup

Ingredients:

1 medium onion, sliced thin
2 stalks celery, sliced
1 tb. crushed garlic
1 tsp. finely diced fresh ginger
2 tbs. olive oil
1 tsp. sesame oil
2 medium carrots, julienne-cut
(matchstick size)
1 lb. sliced mushrooms
1 diced green pepper
1/2 cup soy sauce
1/2 cup brown sugar
1/4 head cabbage, thin-sliced
3 quarts water

Instructions:

In a 6-quart pot sauté the onion, celery, garlic, and ginger in the olive oil and sesame oil for 10 minutes on medium heat until tender. Add all other ingredients. Stir until sugar dissolves. Bring to a boil and simmer for one hour.

Yield: 4 quarts; serves 6-8.

20

Australian Cabbage Soup

Ingredients:

1 medium onion, diced
3 stalks celery, diced
2 tbs. crushed garlic
2 tbs. olive oil
1 lb. mushrooms, sliced
2 large potatoes, diced
1 small head cabbage, shredded
3 quarts water
2 tbs. mushroom base
salt to taste
black pepper to taste
1 1/2 cups roux (page 2)

Instructions:

In a large soup kettle sauté the onion, celery, and garlic in the olive oil for 10 minutes on medium heat until tender. Add all other ingredients except roux. Bring to a boil and simmer for 45 minutes. Slowly blend in roux until it dissolves and soup thickens. Simmer for another 15 minutes.

Yield: 4 quarts; serves 6-8.

German Pork Noodle Soup

Ingredients:

1 medium onion, diced
1 tb. crushed garlic
1 red pepper, diced (optional)
3 stalks celery, diced
2 tbs. olive oil
1 lb. cooked pork butt or
shoulder, diced
1 tb. beef base
1 tb. chicken base
3 quarts water
2 cups apple cider or juice
salt to taste
black pepper to taste
1 1/2 cups roux (page 2)
3 cups of cooked elbow noodles,
penne, or bowties

Instructions:

In a 6-quart pot, sauté the onion, garlic, diced red pepper, and celery in the olive oil for 10 minutes on medium heat until tender. Add all other ingredients except the roux and pasta noodles. Bring to a boil and simmer for one hour. Slowly blend in roux until it dissolves and soup thickens. Simmer for another 15 minutes. Add cooked pasta noodles and simmer for an additional 5 minutes.

Yield: 5 quarts; serves 6-8.

Corn Chowder

Ingredients:

1 medium onion, diced
4 medium carrots, sliced
3 stalks celery, diced
2 tbs. olive oil
2 large potatoes, peeled and diced
1 medium green pepper, diced
4 cups frozen corn
3 quarts water
salt to taste
pepper to taste
2 tbs. parsley
6 dashes Tabasco sauce
1 1/2 cups roux (page 2)
1 cup milk

Instructions:

In a 6-quart pot, sauté the onion, carrots, and celery in the olive oil on medium heat for 10 minutes until tender. Add all other ingredients except the roux and milk. Bring to a boil. Simmer for 45 minutes on low heat. Add roux and stir until thoroughly blended. Add milk and stir into the mixture. Simmer another 15 minutes on low heat.

Yield: 4 quarts; serves 6-8.

Hungarian Bean Soup

Ingredients:
2 tbs. olive oil
1 tb. crushed garlic
4 medium carrots, sliced
3 stalks celery, diced
1 medium onion, diced
1 small head cabbage, chopped
2 large potatoes, diced
1 tb. horseradish
2 tbs. vegetable base
3 quarts water
salt to taste
black pepper to taste
1-24 oz. jar of cooked white beans

Instructions:
In a 6-quart pot, sauté in olive oil the garlic, carrots, celery, and onion for 10 minutes on medium heat until tender. Add all other ingredients except beans. Bring to a boil and simmer for one hour. Add jar of beans and simmer for 10 minutes.

Yield: 4 quarts; serves 6-8.

Garden Vegetable Soup

Ingredients:
4 medium carrots, sliced
1 medium onion, diced
1 tb. crushed garlic
4 stalks celery, diced
2 tbs. olive oil
1 lb. sliced mushrooms
2 large potatoes, peeled and diced
1 14-oz. can diced tomatoes
1 cup frozen peas
1 cup frozen corn
1 tb. dried oregano
1 tb. dried basil
4 quarts water
2 tbs. vegetable base
salt to taste
black pepper to taste

Instructions:
In a 6-quart pot, sauté the carrots, onion, garlic, and celery in the olive oil for 10 minutes on medium heat until tender. Add all other ingredients. Bring to a boil and simmer for one hour.

Yield: 5 quarts; serves 6-8.

"a sensible habit"

Irish Cabbage Soup

Ingredients:
1 medium onion, diced
4 medium carrots, sliced
1 tb. crushed garlic
3 stalks celery, diced
2 tbs. olive oil
1 small head cabbage, shredded
2 large potatoes, diced
1 tb. dried parsley
3 quarts water
2 tbs. vegetable base
salt to taste
white pepper to taste
1 1/2 cup roux (page 2)
2 cups milk

Instructions:
In a large soup kettle, sauté the onion, carrots, garlic, and celery in the olive oil for 10 minutes on medium heat until tender. Add all other ingredients except milk and roux. Bring to a boil, then simmer for one hour. Blend roux into soup until it thoroughly dissolves. Simmer for 15 minutes, stirring every five minutes until soup thickens. Stir in milk and simmer for an additional 10 minutes.

Yield: 4 quarts; serves 6-8.

Salads

We usually associate salads with vegetables, but salads can be made from a wide variety of ingredients. The key to making good salads is to use super-fresh ingredients. In winter, we depend on the supermarket for fresh fruits and vegetables, but during the harvest season we are lucky to have farmers' markets and buyers' coops throughout the state, where the fruits and vegetables come direct from the grower to you. Here in Madison, there is a farmers' market twice a week. Even if you can't make it to the farmers' market, try to buy your salad ingredients the same day you make your salad. You'll notice the difference!

Grilled Chicken Salad

Ingredients:

4 5-oz. (approx.) boneless, skinless
chicken breasts
1/4 cup olive oil
1 head Romaine lettuce, cleaned
and chopped
1/4 thin-sliced red onion
4 large, fresh mushrooms, cleaned
and sliced
2 fresh tomatoes, wedge-sliced
2 oz. crumbled Feta cheese
lemon-vinaigrette (see
recipe, page 35)

Instructions:

In a pan, sauté the chicken breasts in olive oil on moderate heat for 5 minutes on each side. Remove from pan and slice each breast into thin strips. On 4 large dinner plates, make a bed of lettuce. Arrange the red onions, mushrooms, and tomato wedges on the lettuce. Place the strips of sautéed chicken breast on top. Sprinkle the Feta cheese around the plate. Dress with lemon vinaigrette.

Serves 4.

Gotta getta chicken salad!

Greek Salad

Ingredients for dressing:
1/2 cup olive oil
1/2 cup lemon juice
1 tsp. basil
1 tsp. oregano
1 tsp. salt
1 tsp. ground black pepper

Salad ingredients:
1 head Romaine lettuce, cleaned
and chopped
2 12-oz. cans of drained,
quartered artichokes
1 cucumber, peeled, quartered
lengthwise, and cut in 1/2" slices
1 small red onion, sliced
1 red pepper, sliced and chopped
4 chopped green onions
4 oz. drained capers
8 oz. crumbled Feta cheese
16 kalamata olives

Instructions:
In a blender or food processor, mix the olive oil, lemon juice, basil, oregano, salt, and pepper for one minute. Place all salad ingredients except the Feta cheese and kalamata olives in a bowl and toss with the dressing. Place the mixed salad on 4 large dinner plates. Spread the Feta cheese crumbles and olives atop the salads.
Serves 4.

Chef Salad

Ingredients:

1 head Romaine lettuce, cleaned
and chopped
1/2 thin-sliced red onion
10 oz. frozen or fresh asparagus spears,
lightly steamed
1 can whole pitted large black olives
2 tomatoes cut into 8 wedges each
2 hard boiled eggs, each peeled
and cut into 6 wedges
4 oz. capers
8 oz. sliced turkey or ham,
cut into narrow strips
1 cup lemon vinaigrette dressing
(see recipe, page 35)

Instructions:

On a large dinner plate, form a bed with the Romaine lettuce. Spread the red onions, asparagus, olives, tomato wedges, egg wedges, and capers on the bed of lettuce. Arrange the strips of ham or turkey on top. Dress with lemon vinaigrette.

Serves 4.

Salad Niçoise

Ingredients:

1 head Romaine lettuce, cleaned
and chopped
4 4-oz. thin-sliced and grilled
fresh tuna steaks
11 oz. fresh green beans
2 medium tomatoes sliced into
8 wedges per tomato
2 cups red potatoes, steamed, cooled,
and sliced
2 hard-boiled eggs, peeled and each cut
into 8 wedges
16 kalamata or black olives
1/2 cup lemon vinaigrette dressing (see
recipe, page 35)
additional salt and black pepper to taste

Instructions:

For each salad, place chopped lettuce on large dinner plate. Place whole
cooked tuna steak in center of the bed of
lettuce. Spread green beans, potato,
tomato and egg wedges, and black olives
around the edges of the lettuce bed and
around the tuna steak. Sprinkle generous
portions of shaken vinaigrette dressing
over all the ingredients except the tuna.

Makes 4 salads.

Mandarin Beef Salad
(or Pork, Chicken, or Turkey)

Ingredients:

1/2 cup cold water

1-15 oz. can drained mandarin oranges (save liquid in a separate bowl)

1 tb. balsamic vinegar

1 tb. soy sauce

1 tb. cornstarch

1 head Romaine lettuce, cleaned and chopped

1 small sliced onion

1/4 head thin-sliced red cabbage

2 small raw carrots, cut julienne-style (like matchsticks)

1 lb. thin-sliced cooked roast beef (pork, chicken, or turkey may be substituted)

Instructions for mandarin salad dressing:

In a small sauce pan bring the 1/2 cup of water and drained mandarin juice to a boil. Add the balsamic vinegar and soy sauce and again bring to a boil. Mix the cornstarch in a small amount of water and blend until it dissolves into a smooth liquid. Slowly add to the boiling mixture while stirring until the ingredients in the pan thicken. Simmer for three minutes until the dressing is cooked (translucent). Allow to cool.

Instructions for salad:

For each salad, on large dinner plate, arrange chopped lettuce. Place sliced onions, cabbage, and julienned carrots on the bed of lettuce. Arrange thin strips of roast beef on top of the vegetables. Arrange mandarin oranges on top. Dress.

Makes 4 salads.

Turkey Salad

Ingredients:

2 stalks celery, chopped
1/2 cup chopped dill pickles
1/2 cup diced red pepper
1 lb. finely diced, cooked turkey breast
1 cup mayonnaise
2 tbs. Dijon mustard
2 tbs. sour cream
3-4 dashes Tabasco sauce
salt and pepper to taste
1 head Romaine lettuce, cleaned
and chopped
1/2 lb. red seedless grapes
12 honeydew melon slices
4 Kaiser rolls

Instructions:

Place all ingredients except lettuce, fruits, and Kaiser rolls into a 4-quart bowl until thoroughly mixed. Form a bed of chopped lettuce on a large dinner plate. Put 2-3 large spoonfuls of turkey mix in the center of the bed of lettuce. Garnish with a generous portion of melon and grapefruit slices. If making a sandwich, slice Kaiser roll in half and put 2 large tablespoons of turkey salad on the roll and garnish plate with melon and grapes.

Serves 4.

Salad Dressings

Raspberry Vinaigrette Dressing

Ingredients:

3/4 cup fresh or frozen raspberries
1/4 cup honey
2 eggs
2 tbs. Dijon mustard
1/2 tsp. black ground pepper
1/2 tsp. salt
1 cup red wine vinegar
2 cups apple cider vinegar
1/2 cup salad oil
1 tb. olive oil

Instructions:

Blend all ingredients except olive oil thoroughly in a blender or food processor for one minute.

Pour into a glass or stainless steel bowl. Slowly drizzle olive oil while stirring with a whisk or French whip.

Yield: 4 1/4 cups.

Buttermilk Ranch Dressing

Ingredients:

1/2 lb. sour cream
1 cup mayonnaise
3/4 tb. garlic powder
1/2 tb. dried dill weed
1/2 tb. dried parsley
1/2 tb. dried chives
1/2 tsp. salt
2 dashes Tabasco sauce
2 cups of buttermilk

Instructions:

Blend all ingredients in a food processor or with a hand whisk. If you use only 1 1/2 cups of buttermilk the mixture will be stiffer and suitable as a vegetable dip. This dressing can also be used on French fries or as a marinade for baked chicken.

Yield: 4 1/2 cups.

Low-Fat Cucumber Dressing

Ingredients:

3 cups plain lowfat yogurt
5/8 cup lowfat mayonnaise
juice from 1/2 fresh lemon
1/2 tb. dried dill
1 tsp. dried oregano
1 tsp. dried basil
2 dashes Tabasco sauce
1/4 finely minced medium red onion
1/2 finely chopped, peeled and seeded,
cucumber
1/8 cup crushed garlic

Instructions:

Combine all ingredients in a blender or food processor for one minute.

Yield: 5 cups.

This dressing is a natural on lettuce salad and great on Greek foods. It's also a complement to spicy Thai and Indian recipes.

Lemon Vinaigrette

Ingredients:

2 tbs. crushed garlic
1/2 cup Lea and Perrins
Worcestershire Sauce
1/4 cup red wine vinegar
1 cup lemon juice
2 tbs. dried basil
2 tbs. dried oregano
1 tb. black ground pepper
1/2 tsp. salt
1 1/2 cups salad oil
2 cups olive oil

Instructions:

Mix all ingredients except olive oil in a blender or food processor for one minute. Pour into bowl. Slowly drizzle the olive oil into the mix while stirring with a whisk or French whip. Let stand for 30 minutes for flavors to meld.

Yield: 5 cups.

Chipotle Mayonnaise Dressing

Ingredients:

2 cups mayonnaise

2 tbs. cumin

2 tbs. fresh lemon juice

2 tbs. honey

2 tbs. freshly chopped cilantro

1/2 tsp. crushed garlic

3 drained, chopped chipotle peppers

1/4 tsp. salt

Instructions:

Mix all ingredients into a blender or food processor for one minute.

Yield: 5 cups.

The Blue Plate Diner uses this dressing to perk up our grilled tuna steak sandwich. The dressing is also great on a taco salad or as a veggie dip. The key ingredient is chipotle peppers, which have a hot smoky flavor. They may be purchased in cans from most Mexican grocery stores.

French Dressing

Ingredients:

14 oz. ketchup

1/4 medium finely chopped onion

6 oz. apple cider vinegar

3/8 cup sugar

juice from 1/2 fresh lemon

1 1/2 tsp. paprika

1/4 tsp. white pepper

1 tsp. garlic powder

1 tsp. onion powder

2 dashes Tabasco sauce

3/4 cup vegetable oil

Instructions:

Mix all ingredients in a blender or food processor for one minute.

Yield: 5 cups.

Big Bowls

Big Bowls

everal years ago, Monty found some blue bowls that hold 32 ounces. That's a quart and that's a big bowl. He thought it would be a good idea to have a series of one-dish meals served in these big blue bowls, one special each day Thus the "Big Bowl Special" was born. Now, regular customers routinely ask, "What's the Big Bowl today?" It can be almost any kind of stew or casserole, or some hearty concoction over rice, couscous, barley, or noodles. Sometimes it's a Big Bowl of fish and chips, or, if Tim is in a Cajun mood, a spicy Jambalaya. Because the Big Bowl can be almost anything, it gives Tim carte blanche to exercise his creative impulses. One day, he might be inspired to do Moroccan chicken, cooked with garbanzo beans, on another, Sao Paulo pork with peppery spices and tomato. Tim can take some of mom's old favorites—tuna casserole or macaroni and cheese—and give them just a little twist to make them special. In this chapter you will find just a small sampling of Tim's Big Bowls. Others have yet to be invented, and you'll just have to come to the diner to discover them for yourself.

BEST YOU EVER ATE

CHILI

Wild Turkey

Ingredients for rices:
1 cup wild rice
1 tb. olive oil
3 cups water

1 cup white rice
1 tb. olive oil
2 cups water

Ingredients for turkey mixture
2 cups mushrooms, sliced
1 medium onion, diced
3 stalks celery, diced
1 tb. crushed fresh garlic
2 tbs. olive oil
4 cups water
1/2 cup roux (page 2)
1 lb. turkey breast, diced
1 cup milk
1 tb. chicken base
salt to taste
pepper to taste
1/2 oz. Wild Turkey bourbon (optional)
Tabasco sauce to taste

Instructions:
Cook wild rice in a 2-quart sauce pan with water and olive oil for 1 1/4 hours.

In a 6-quart pan, sauté the mushrooms, onion, celery, and garlic in olive oil on low heat until tender. Add 4 cups of water and bring to a boil. Slowly add the roux and blend with a whisk or French whip until the mixture thickens. Add the diced turkey. Stir in the milk, chicken base, salt, pepper, bourbon, and Tabasco until well blended. Simmer 5 minutes while starting second pan of rice to boil.

In another 2-quart sauce pan, bring 2 cups of water to a boil. Add the white rice, olive oil, and salt. Cover and simmer on low heat for 15 minutes.

After both rices are cooked, combine them with the Wild Turkey mixture. Serve in a big bowl.

Serves 6-8.

Rice & Pinto Beans

Ingredients:

2 quarts water
2 cups dried pinto beans
3 stalks celery, diced
1 medium onion, diced
1 green pepper, diced
1 tb. cumin
1 tb. chili powder
1 tb. Dijon mustard
1 tb. ketchup
1 diced, fresh jalapeno pepper
Tabasco sauce to taste
salt to taste
black pepper to taste
4 cups water
salt to taste
1 tb. olive oil
2 cups white rice

Instructions:

In a 6-quart pot, place 2 quarts water, pinto beans, celery, onion, and green pepper and bring to a boil. Cook for 2-3 hours until the beans are soft. Add the cumin, chili powder, Dijon mustard, ketchup, jalapeno, Tabasco sauce, salt, and black pepper and stir well into the bean and vegetable mixture.

Separately, during the last half hour as the beans are cooking, heat to boil the 4 cups of water, salt, and olive oil. When water boils, place rice into the pan, stir, and reduce heat. Cover the pan and cook rice according to package instructions.

Place rice into big bowls. Top with pinto beans.

Serves 4-6.

"a sensible habit"

Moroccan Chicken

Ingredients:
3 cups water
2 cups dry couscous
1 medium onion, diced
2 cups sliced mushrooms
3 stalks celery, diced
2 medium carrots, sliced
1 diced red pepper
2 cups coarsely chopped cabbage
2 cloves garlic, crushed
2 tbs. olive oil
3 cups water
1/2 cup red balsamic vinegar
1 cup cooked and drained
garbanzo beans
1/4 cup roux(page 2)
1 lb. boneless chicken breast,
cooked and diced
salt to taste
black pepper to taste
Tabasco sauce to taste

Instructions:
In a bowl combine 3 cups of hot, but not boiling, water with 2 cups of dried couscous. Stir together, cover, and allow to stand in bowl for 10 minutes. In a 6-quart pot, sauté onion, mushrooms, celery, carrots, red pepper, cabbage, and garlic in the olive oil on medium heat for 15 minutes until tender. Add 3 cups hot water, balsamic vinegar, and garbanzo beans and simmer until the mixture boils. Reduce heat and stir in the roux until it dissolves and the mixture thickens. Simmer 10 minutes. Add the chicken, salt, black pepper, and Tabasco sauce. Stir until blended. Put couscous into big bowls and top with the Moroccan chicken.

Serves 4-6.

Taboule

Dressing ingredients:
3/4 cup balsamic vinegar
1 tb. olive oil
1/4 cup honey
6 dashes Tabasco sauce

Taboule ingredients:
6 cups very hot water
4 cups dry couscous
1 carrot, peeled and finely diced
1/2 medium onion, finely diced
2 medium tomatoes, finely diced
1/4 cup finely chopped fresh mint
1/2 cup finely chopped fresh parsley
salt to taste

Instructions for dressing:
Mix the balsamic vinegar, olive oil, honey, and Tabasco sauce in a bowl with a whisk for two minutes and set aside.

Instructions for taboule:
In a 6-quart bowl, place the hot water and couscous. Cover and hold for 10 minutes. Mix the carrot, onion, tomatoes, mint, parsley, and salt with the couscous. Add the dressing and stir into Taboule. Serve in a big bowl.
Serves 4-6.

Sao Paulo Pork

Ingredients:

1 1/2 to 2 lbs. boneless loin
or butt of pork
1 medium onion, diced
1 14-oz. can diced tomatoes
1 tb. cumin
1 tb. chili powder
salt to taste
6 dashes Tabasco sauce
4 cups water
2 cups white rice
1 tb. olive oil
salt to taste

Instructions:

Roast the pork in the oven for 2 hours at 350 degrees. Cool until the pork can be cut into 1" diced chunks. Place them into a 4-quart sauce pan. Add the onion and tomatoes. Simmer for 2-3 hours until the pork is so tender that it's shredding and falling apart. (During the 2-3 hour simmer, add water as needed so that the mixture will not dry out and scorch.) Add the cumin, chili powder, salt, and Tabasco sauce and simmer 15 additional minutes. While the pork is simmering for the last 15 minutes, bring the 4 cups of water to a boil in a separate 2-quart sauce pan. Add the rice, olive oil, and salt to taste to the boiling water. Cover with a lid and simmer on low heat for 15 minutes. Pour Sao Paulo pork over rice in a big bowl.

Serves 6-8.

  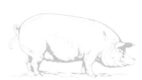

Turkey Divan

Ingredients:

1 medium onion, diced
2 cups sliced mushrooms
2 cups chopped broccoli
2 cloves garlic, crushed
2 tbs. olive oil
1 lb. cooked and diced turkey breast
2 cups water
1/4 cup roux (page 37)
1 tb. chicken base
1 tb. mushroom base
salt to taste
black pepper
1 cup milk
4 cups water
white pepper
1 tb. olive oil
2 cups white rice

Instructions:

In a 6-quart pot sauté the onion, mushrooms, broccoli, and garlic in the olive oil for 10 minutes on medium heat until tender. Add the cooked turkey breast and water to the vegetables. Bring to a boil. Stir in the roux until it dissolves and the mixture thickens. Simmer 10 minutes. Add the chicken base, mushroom base, salt and black pepper. Stir in the milk. Blend all ingredients.

Separately, heat to a boil the 4 cups of water, salt, white pepper, and olive oil. When the water boils, place rice into the pan and stir. Cover the pan with a lid, reduce heat, and cook rice according to package instructions. Place rice into big bowls and top with the turkey mixture.

Serves 4-6.

43

Tuna Casserole

Ingredients:

2 stalks celery, chopped
1 medium onion, diced
2 cups sliced mushrooms
1 tb. crushed garlic
2 tbs. olive oil
4 cups water
1/2 cup roux (page 2)
1 cup milk
1 cup sour cream
2 cups frozen and defrosted green peas
1 12-oz. can of white tuna
1 lb. cooked (al dente) pasta (penne, elbow noodles, or other pasta)
8 oz. grated cheddar cheese
1 cup crushed potato chips

Instructions:

In a 6-quart pot sauté the celery, onion, mushrooms, and garlic in the olive oil on medium heat for 10 minutes until tender. Add water and bring to a boil. Stir in roux until it dissolves and the mixture thickens. Simmer 10 minutes. Stir in the milk, sour cream, peas, and flaked tuna. Bring to a boil. Pour over pasta in a big bowl. Garnish with cheddar cheese and crushed potato chips.

Serves 4-6.

Macaroni & Cheese

Ingredients:

3 1/2 cups whole milk, half-and-half,
or cream
1/4 cup roux (page 2)
2 cups shredded Parmesan
or Asiago cheese
4 cups shredded cheddar cheese
1 tb. Dijon mustard
Tabasco sauce to taste
1 lb. elbow noodles
salt to taste

Instructions:

In a 6-quart pot, heat the milk, half-and-half, or cream (do not boil or it will burn). Stir in the roux until it dissolves, constantly stirring with a whisk until there is a smooth white sauce. Add all the other ingredients except the elbow noodles, stirring them until they blend into a smooth sauce. Cook elbow noodles, place into big bowls, and top with the sauce.

Serves 4-6.

It's so wholesome!

Cajun Turkey Hash

Ingredients:

8 small red potatoes, cooked and diced
1 tb. garlic
3 stalks diced celery
2 cups mushrooms, cut in half
1 diced green pepper
1 diced medium onion
2 tbs. olive oil
2 tbs. Cajun spice (page 62)
1 lb. turkey breast, cooked and cubed
1/2 lb. bacon, fried and crumbled
salt to taste
black pepper to taste
Tabasco sauce to taste

Instructions:

Cook and dice potatoes. Cover and set aside. In a 6-quart pot, sauté garlic, celery, mushrooms, green pepper, and onion in the olive oil on medium heat for 10 minutes until tender. Add Cajun spice and stir into vegetables. Add cubed turkey, crumbled bacon, and diced potatoes. Stir all ingredients in pot. Add salt, pepper, and Tabasco. Stir well. Serve in a big bowl.

Serves 4-6.

Paprikash

Ingredients:

1 medium onion, diced
3 stalks celery, chopped
2 tbs. olive oil
1 28-oz. can tomato sauce
1 tb. mild paprika
1 tb. chicken base
1/2 cup roux (page 2)
1 cup sour cream
1 cup milk
salt to taste
pepper to taste
1 chicken cut up into 8 pieces
1 lb. noodles of your choice

Instructions:

In a 6-quart pot, sauté onion and celery in olive oil on medium heat for 10 minutes until tender. Add tomato sauce, paprika, and chicken base. Simmer for 20 minutes. Add roux and stir until it dissolves and thickens the mixture. Simmer 10 minutes. Stir in the sour cream and milk until it blends into the mixture. Add salt and pepper and simmer for 10 minutes until all ingredients are blended into a sauce.

Cut up chicken and place in a 12" x 13" baking dish. Cover the chicken with sauce. Cover with tin foil and bake in oven for one hour at 350 degrees. Cook noodles. Serve chicken and sauce over noodles in a big bowl.

Serves 4-6.

Greek Rice

Ingredients:

1 medium onion, diced
2 stalks celery, diced
1 tb. crushed garlic
2 cups sliced mushrooms
1 cup sliced black olives
2 tbs. olive oil
2 tbs. oregano
1 cup white wine
1/2 cup finely diced parsley
juice from 2 fresh lemons
salt and pepper

3 cups water
1/2 cup white rice
1 tb. olive oil
8 oz. crumbled Feta cheese

Instructions:

In a 6-quart pan, sauté the onion, celery, garlic, mushrooms, and black olives in the olive oil on low heat for 15 minutes. Add the oregano and wine and simmer for 10 minutes. Add the parsley, lemon juice, salt, and pepper.

In a separate 2-quart sauce pan, bring the 3 cups of water to a boil. Add the rice, olive oil, and salt. Cover with a lid and simmer for 15 minutes. After the rice has cooked, toss it with the sautéed vegetables. Serve in a big bowl and top with Feta cheese crumbles.

Serves 4-6.

Jambalaya

Ingredients:
1 medium onion, diced
2 tbs. crushed garlic cloves
3 stalks celery, diced
1 green pepper, diced
2 tbs. olive oil
8 oz. cooked and diced ham
8 oz. cooked and diced chicken breast
6 slices bacon, fried and crumbled
1 28-oz. can diced tomatoes
juice from 1 fresh squeezed lemon
1 fresh jalapeno pepper, diced
salt to taste
black pepper to taste
Tabasco sauce, to taste

4 cups water
salt to taste
1 tb. olive oil
2 cups white rice

IT'S A HIT

Instructions:
In a 6-quart pot, sauté the onion, garlic, celery, and green pepper in olive oil on medium heat for 10 minutes until tender. Add the ham, chicken, and bacon and stir together with the vegetables. Add the diced tomatoes, lemon juice, jalapeno pepper, salt, pepper, and Tabasco sauce and simmer together for 20 minutes.

Separately, heat to a boil the 4 cups of water, salt, and olive oil. When the water boils, place rice into the pan and stir. Cover, reduce heat, and cook rice according to package instructions. When rice has cooked, blend it together with the sauce of meats and vegetables. Place into big bowls.
Serves 6-8.

Chicken Provençal
(French Chicken Stew)

Ingredients:

2 medium carrots, sliced
2 cups sliced mushrooms
1 medium onion, diced
2 tbs. crushed garlic
3 stalks celery, diced
2 tbs. olive oil
2 quarts water
8 red potatoes, washed, cooked (with peel), and quartered
1 tb. chicken base
1 lb. boneless chicken breast
1 cup roux (see page 2)
2 tbs. finely chopped parsley
1 lb. of cooked pasta noodles of your choice

Instructions:

In a 6-quart pot, sauté carrots, mushrooms, onion, garlic, and celery in olive oil for 10 minutes on medium heat. Add water, potatoes, and chicken base and bring to a boil. Simmer for one hour until vegetables are tender. While vegetables are boiling, preheat oven to 400 degrees. Bake chicken breasts in a shallow pan in oven for 7 minutes. Remove chicken breasts from oven, cool, and cut into 1" cubes. When vegetable mixture is tender, stir in roux until it dissolves and the mixture thickens. Add the diced chicken to the thickened vegetable mixture. Serve over noodles in a big bowl. Garnish with finely chopped parsley. **Serves 4-6.**

Thai Noodles

Ingredients:
1 tsp. fresh peeled ginger
1 tsp. fresh garlic
1/4 cup brown sugar
1 jalapeno pepper, finely diced
1/2 medium onion, diced
1 tb. salad oil
juice from 1 fresh lime
1/4 cup finely chopped cilantro
1 /2 tsp. red pepper flakes
1 cup peanut butter
1/2 cup natural coconut milk
(Do not use condensed, sweetened coconut milk)
1 lb. spaghetti or linguine noodles, cooked al dente

Instructions:
Place all ingredients except the peanut butter, coconut milk, and cooked noodles into a blender and puree. Transfer into a 2-quart sauce pan. Add peanut butter. Simmer on low heat until the peanut butter is blended into the mix. Simmer for 5 more minutes while stirring in the coconut milk. Serve over cooked noodles in a big bowl.

Serves 4-6.

Option:

In a frying pan, sauté on low heat in 2 tbs. olive oil, 1 finely diced carrot, 1 medium onion, 1/2 sweet red pepper, and/or 1/4 head finely chopped purple cabbage until tender. Mix into cooked noodles before pouring the Thai peanut sauce over the noodles. You can use one or more of these optional vegetables depending on your taste.

Scalloped Potatoes & Ham

Ingredients:

20 medium red potatoes, peeled,
sliced, and cooked
1 medium onion, diced
1 tb olive oil
2 quarts milk
3/4 cup roux (page 2)
2 tbs. chicken base
1/2 tsp. white pepper
1/2 cup white wine
1 lb. diced ham

Instructions:

Peel and slice potatoes and boil until tender. Remove potatoes from heat, rinse, drain, and hold. In a 6-quart pot, sauté the onion in the olive oil on medium heat for 5 minutes. Add milk and heat, but do not boil. Stir in roux until it dissolves. Simmer until the mixture thickens. Add chicken base, pepper, and white wine and stir until these ingredients are well mixed into the heated and thickened milk. Spread cooked potatoes into a casserole dish. Add ham on top of the potatoes. Pour white sauce over the potatoes and ham. Bake for 1/2 hour at 400 degrees. Remove from oven and cool for 15 minutes. Serve in a big bowl.

Serves 4-6.

52

Beef 'n' Barley

Ingredients for barley:
4 cups water
1 carrot, finely diced
1 medium onion, diced
1/2 lb. sliced mushrooms
1 cup medium barley

Ingredients for beef:
1/2 lb. sliced mushrooms
1 medium onion, diced
2 tbs. olive oil
1 lb. lean beef (flank steak or any lean roast meat) cut into half-inch cubes
4 cups water
1/4 cup roux (page 2)
1 tb. beef base

Instructions:
For barley: In a 2-quart sauce pan with 3 cups of water cook carrot, onion, mushrooms, and barley for about one hour. As the barley cooks and expands add the 4th cup of water. Simmer until the barley is tender.

For beef: In a 4-quart pan, sauté on low heat the mushrooms and onion in olive oil for five minutes. Add the cubed beef and brown the meat for 10 minutes. Add the 4 cups of water and bring to a boil. Slowly stir in the roux until the mixtures thickens into a gravy. Add the beef base and simmer 10 minutes. Place the barley in a big bowl and top with beef in its gravy.

Serves 4-6

Sandwiches

Sandwiches

The secret of a great sandwich is to use fresh ingredients and really good bread, and then not to skimp when putting them together. It used to be hard to find good bread, but it's a lot easier today, since diners have demanded better bread. Of course, it helps to be creative and sensitive in the combining of ingredients, too. At the Blue Plate Diner, Tim has been experimenting and refining his sandwich recipes for many years. Here are some of his favorites, which, not incidentally, are favorites of Blue Plate Diner customers, also.

55

Green Goddess Sandwich

Ingredients:
8 slices toasted wheat bread
4 oz. room-temperature cream cheese
1 small red onion, sliced
12 leaves fresh spinach, cleaned
1 ripe avocado, peeled, pitted, and sliced
4 oz. alfalfa sprouts

Instructions:
Toast the wheat bread and allow it to cool, then spread with cream cheese. On one slice of bread, layer the red onion slices, spinach leaves, and slices of avocado. Top with the alfalfa sprouts.

Makes 4 sandwiches.

Hot Italian Sub

Ingredients:

6-in. French sub roll, sliced lengthwise
2 thin (1/2 oz. each) ham slices
2 thin (1/2 oz. each.) salami slices
2 thin slices red onion
1 peperoncino, diced
1/4 green pepper, sliced
2 slices tomato
2 thin (1/2 oz. each) Provolone
cheese slices
1 large leaf of lettuce
1 tb. lemon vinaigrette (page 35)

Instructions:

Brush inside halves of the roll with the vinaigrette. Place the sliced meats, onion, peperoncino, peppers, and tomato on one half of the roll. Place the cheese on the other half. Place in the oven at 350 degrees for 10 minutes or until the cheese has melted. When the sandwich is removed from the oven, add the lettuce and close.

Makes one sandwich.

It's so tasty!

Artichoke Sandwich

Ingredients:

2 tbs. olive oil
1 medium onion, diced
2 medium leeks, sliced
4 cups sliced mushrooms
8-oz. can artichoke hearts, drained
1 red pepper, diced
4 fresh tomatoes, diced
1/2 cup pine nuts
1 cup commercial pesto sauce
1 oz. soy sauce
4 sub buns
grated Parmesan cheese

Instructions:

Preheat oven to 400 degrees. In a non-stick fry pan, heat the olive oil and sauté the onions and leeks until they caramelize. Add the mushrooms and artichokes and cook for 15 minutes. Add red pepper, tomatoes, pine nuts, and pesto, and stir into the mixture. Cook 5 minutes. Add soy sauce and stir into mixture (**Yields 2 quarts.** This mixture will keep in the refrigerator for several days and may also be used over pasta or rice.) Spread mixture over a sub bun. Sprinkle Parmesan cheese on the open sandwich. Bake at 400 degrees for 10 minutes in a preheated oven.

Yields 8 open-face sandwiches. Serves 4.

The Sheldon Sandwich
(Vegetarian Reuben)

Marinade ingredients:
1/2 cup fresh minced garlic
2 cups soy sauce
2 cups white vinegar
2 tsp. white pepper
1/2 cup honey
2 tb. fresh minced ginger

Instructions for marinade:
Mix all ingredients. Cut tofu into 1/4 inch slices. Cover with marinade overnight. When ready to use, drain marinade into container and preserve. This marinade keeps for weeks in the refrigerator. It is also good for vegetable and stir-fries.

Yields 5 cups.

Sandwich ingredients:
8 slices rye bread
1 lb. tofu
4 1-oz. slices Swiss cheese
16 oz. can sauerkraut, well-drained
8 slices tomato

To make sandwich:
Brush one side of each slice of bread with oil. Place 4 slices, oil side down, in a non-stick pan under low heat. Place the marinated tofu, Swiss cheese, sauerkraut, and two slices of tomato on top of each slice of bread in the pan. Place the other 4 slices on top, oil side up. Fry the sandwich under low heat until the bread on bottom is browned. With a spatula, flip the sandwich and brown the other side.

Makes 4 sandwiches.

Monty Cristo Sandwich

Ingredients:
1 cup milk
1 large egg
8 slices cinnamon bread
4 1-oz. slices ham
4 1-oz. slices turkey
4 1-oz. slices Swiss cheese

Instructions:
Make a French toast batter by whipping thoroughly the milk and egg. Dip one side of four bread slices in the batter and pan-fry as you would French toast. As they are frying, place the slices of meat and cheese on top of each of these slices. Then dip the other four slices, one side only, and place on top, dipped side up, to form the other half of the sandwiches. Flip each sandwich over so that the other side can brown. Serve with honey mustard or cranberry relish.

Makes 4 sandwiches.

T. N. T. (Vegetarian B.L.T.)

Marinade ingredients:
1/4 cup mustard seed
1/4 cup fennel seed
1/4 cup cumin seed
2 cups soy sauce
3 cups water
2 tsp. onion powder
2 tsp. garlic powder
juice from 1 lemon
juice from 1 lime
1/2 cup maple syrup
1/4 cup honey
1 1/2 cup apple cider
1 tsp. liquid smoke

Other ingredients:
1 lb. tempe
4 leaves lettuce
8 slices tomato
4 Kaiser rolls

Instructions:

Mix the mustard, fennel, and cumin seeds in a dry frying pan and roast for 15 minutes. In another bowl mix the soy sauce, water, onion and garlic powders, juices from the squeezed lemon and lime, maple syrup, honey, apple cider, and liquid smoke. After thoroughly mixed, add the seeds. Cut the tempe into 1/4" slices and place them in a shallow baking pan. Pour enough of the marinade mixture over the tempe so that it is just covered. (Some marinade will remain.) Bake for 1 1/2 hours at 220 degrees. Tempe will slowly absorb the marinade and should come out of the oven dry. Place a slice of tempe in a sliced Kaiser roll topped with lettuce and tomato.

Makes 4 sandwiches.

Cajun Chicken Sandwich

Cajun spice mix ingredients:
1 cup paprika
1/4 cup cayenne pepper
2 tb. salt
2 tb. oregano
1 tb. thyme
2 tb. black pepper
2 tb. white pepper
2 tb. onion powder
2 tb. garlic powder

Other ingredients:
4 5-oz. boneless, skinless chicken breasts
4 leaves lettuce
8 slices tomato
4 Kaiser rolls

Instructions for Cajun spice mix:
(This recipe will make enough spice mix for this recipe with plenty left over for other uses in the future.) In a bowl, mix all ingredients thoroughly. Store in a small, air-tight jar or spice container.

Instructions for cooking the chicken:
Dip the chicken pieces in the spice mix on both sides, then grill or fry under low heat until they are cooked through. Serve on sliced Kaiser rolls with lettuce and tomato.

Makes 4 sandwiches.

Black Bean Burger

Ingredients:

2 cups of cooked or 14-oz. can black
beans, drained
3/8 cup of your favorite salsa
1 egg
1 1/2 tsp. apple cider vinegar
1/2 cup wheat flour
1/8 cup corn meal
3/4 tsp. salt
3/4 tsp. black pepper
2 tbs. olive oil
12 slices tomato
6 lettuce leaves
6 Kaiser rolls

Instructions:

Thoroughly mix black beans with salsa, eggs, and vinegar. Add the wheat flour, corn meal, salt, and pepper to yield 4 cups. Mix and stir until ingredients are well blended. Form into 4-oz. round patties. Place olive oil in a non-stick frying pan on low heat. Place formed patties into the heated pan and cook until firm and brown on one side. Flip and fry until brown on the other side. Serve on a sliced Kaiser roll. Garnish with lettuce and sliced tomatoes.

Makes 6 sandwiches.

Shredded Pork Sandwich

6-8 Kaiser rolls

Ingredients to prepare the pork:
2 lbs. boneless pork shoulder, butt,
or loin
2 cups apple cider
14-oz. can diced tomatoes
14 oz. water
salt

**Ingredients for
Tim's barbecue sauce:**
1 medium onion, diced
2 cups apple vinegar
1 cup brown sugar
1 tb. molasses
1 tb. Dijon mustard
1/4 cup Worcestershire sauce
1/2 tsp. cayenne
1 cup tomato paste
5 dashes Tabasco sauce
juice from one lemon
6 oz. ketchup
salt
1 drop liquid smoke (optional)

To cook the pork:
Place the pork in a shallow pan. Add 2 cups of apple cider. Bake for 2 hours at 300 degrees. Remove, cool, and cut the roast into chunks. Place into an 8-quart soup pot with a lid. Add the diced tomatoes and water. Salt to taste. Cover and simmer for 2 additional hours until the meat shreds. Add additional water as needed during this process so as not to scorch the meat. Remove the meat and place into a mixing bowl. Add your favorite barbecue sauce, or use Tim's recipe which has no preservatives or other chemical additives, and toss a little at a time until you like the consistency.
Makes 6-8 sandwiches.

**Instructions for
Tim's barbecue sauce:**

Combine 1/2 the diced onion, vinegar, and brown sugar. Reduce by boiling for 20 minutes. Add the molasses, mustard, Worcestershire sauce, tomato paste, cayenne, and Tabasco sauce. Simmer for an additional 15 minutes. Add the lemon juice, ketchup, and the other half of the onion. Simmer for another 15 minutes.

Yield: 1 quart.

Roasted Veggie Sub

Ingredients:
1/4 cup balsamic vinegar
2 tbs. honey
1 small zucchini
4 quarter-inch slices of red onion
4 quarter-inch slices of green pepper
4 thick slices of tomato
2 oz. sliced Feta cheese
6-in. French sub roll

Instructions:
Mix together the balsamic vinegar and the honey. Slice the zucchini lengthwise into quarters. Slice the red onion, pepper, and tomato into thick slices. Place the sliced vegetables in a small baking pan and pour the balsamic/honey mixture over them. Bake the vegetables for 20 minutes at 400 degrees. Remove from oven. Slice the sub roll in half lengthwise and fill with the baked vegetables. Top with the slices of Feta cheese. Wrap the sandwich in tinfoil. Bake for 10-15 minutes at 400 degrees.

Makes one sandwich.

Pastas & Entrées

Pastas & Entrées

These pasta recipes may be made with the pasta of your choice. The most popular include spaghetti, penne, rotini, bowties, and fettuccini. Buy a good-quality pasta, because the difference in price is small while the difference in quality can be great.

Pasta has the best texture when cooked al dente, to a state of firmness but not mushiness. While cooking pasta, follow the instructions on the package. Test the pasta before the allotted cooking time passes, since it can overcook very quickly. The window for cooking al dente pasta can be up to five minutes with a good-quality pasta, but perhaps only a minute with one of lower quality.

Here is a basic recipe for cooking pasta.

Fill a 6-quart pot with 4 quarts of water. Add one tablespoon of salt and one tablespoon of olive oil and bring to a rapid boil. Place one pound of the pasta of your choice into the rapidly boiling water. Note the recommended cooking time on the pasta package. Several minutes before the allotted cooking time, test the pasta to see whether it has reached al dente. Do not walk away from the pasta, since you could become involved in another cooking chore, resulting in over-cooking. When the pasta tests al dente, remove it immediately from the stove, take it to the sink, run cold water over it to stop the cooking process, and pour it into a colander. Run hot tap water over the pasta to remove excess cooking starch. Drain the pasta in the colander for two minutes. Pour it back into the warm pan and stir in two tablespoons of olive oil. Serve as quickly as possible, since hot pasta will continue to cook if held.

Pasta Faggoli

Ingredients:
1 tb. olive oil
1 medium onion, diced
1 tb. fresh crushed garlic
1/2 sweet green pepper, diced
14-oz. can cooked white navy beans
28-oz. can tomato sauce
1 tb. dried oregano
1 tb. dried basil
1 tb. salt
1 tb. molasses
1 tb. brown sugar
1/2 cup grated Cheddar cheese

Instructions:
In a 4-quart pot, in olive oil, sauté the onion, garlic, and green pepper over medium heat until tender. Add the white beans, tomato sauce, oregano, basil, and salt. Simmer for one hour. Add the molasses, brown sugar, and Cheddar cheese. Simmer for 15 minutes. Serve sauce over your favorite pasta.

Serves 4-6.

Mushroom Tetrazzini

Ingredients:

2 tbs. olive oil
1 tb. fresh crushed garlic
2 stalks celery, diced
1 medium onion, diced
1 lb. sliced mushrooms
1/2 sweet green pepper, diced
8 cups water
1 cup roux (page 2)
1 cup milk or cream
salt and pepper to taste
1/2 cup sour cream
1 cup shredded Parmesan cheese
1 tb. vegetable or mushroom base
1 lb. pasta of your choice

Instructions:

In a 6-quart pot, in olive oil, sauté the garlic, celery, onion, mushrooms, and green pepper on low heat until the vegetables are tender. Add the water and bring to a boil. Stir in the roux until it dissolves and the mixture thickens. Stir the milk or cream into the thickened sauce. Add salt and pepper to taste. Stir in the sour cream, shredded Parmesan cheese, and vegetable or mushroom base. Simmer for 10 minutes while stirring often. In a pasta bowl serve the hot pasta topped with the mushroom tetrazzini sauce.

Serves 4-6.

Tuna Milano

Ingredients:

1 tb. olive oil
1 tb. fresh crushed garlic
1/2 green pepper, chopped
1 medium onion, diced
2 cups sliced mushrooms
1/2 tb. dried basil
1/2 tb. dried oregano
28-oz. can tomato sauce
14-oz. can diced tomatoes
6 1/2-oz. can tuna, drained
2 cups green olives, sliced
juice of one lemon
1/2 cup grated fresh Asiago or
Parmesan cheese
1 lb. pasta

Instructions:

In a 4-quart pot, in olive oil, sauté the garlic, green pepper, onion, and mushrooms over medium heat for 15 minutes until tender. Add the basil and oregano and stir. Add the tomato sauce and diced tomatoes and simmer for 20 minutes. Add the tuna and green olives. Simmer 5 minutes more. Stir in lemon juice and grated cheese. Simmer an additional 5 minutes. Serve in pasta bowl over your favorite pasta.

Serves 4-6

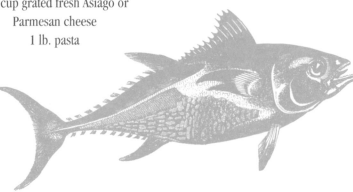

Beef Ragout (Ragu)

Ingredients:
1 tb. olive oil
1 tb. fresh crushed garlic
1 medium onion, diced
1 small green pepper, diced
1 lb. cooked ground beef or
shredded roast beef
14-oz. can diced tomatoes
28-oz. can tomato sauce
1 tb. dried oregano
1 tb. dried fennel
1 tb. sugar
1 tsp salt
1 tb. beef base
1 lb. pasta
fresh grated Parmesan cheese

Instructions:
In a 4-quart pot, in olive oil, sauté the garlic, onion, and green pepper over medium heat for 10 minutes until tender. Add all the other ingredients. Simmer for 30 minutes. Serve over your favorite pasta. Garnish with freshly grated Parmesan cheese.
Serves 4-6.

Marinara with Pasta

Ingredients:
2 tb. olive oil
1 tb. fresh crushed garlic
1 medium onion, diced
1 lb. sliced mushrooms
1 sweet green pepper, finely diced
1/2 cup red wine
1 tb. dried oregano
1 tb. dried basil
1 tb. brown sugar
28-oz. can tomato sauce
14 oz. diced tomatoes
salt and pepper to taste
1 cup Parmesan or Romano cheese
1 lb. pasta
fresh basil (optional)

Instructions:
In a 6-quart pot, in olive oil, sauté the garlic, onion, mushrooms, and green pepper on low heat until the vegetables are tender. Add all the other ingredients except the cheese, pasta, and fresh basil. Bring to a boil. Cover the pot with a lid and reduce heat. Simmer for 30 minutes. Cook the pasta and top with marinara sauce. Sprinkle with Parmesan or Romano cheese. Garnish with fresh basil, if available.

Yields 6 cups sauce.
Serves 4-6.

Mushroom Marinara

Ingredients:
1 tb. olive oil
1 medium onion, diced
1 tb. crushed garlic
1 quart sliced mushrooms
1 tb. dried basil
1 tsp. soy sauce
28-oz. can tomato sauce
14-oz. can diced tomatoes
1/2 tsp. salt
1 tb. sugar
1/2 cup fresh grated Asiago or
Parmesan cheese
1 lb. pasta

Instructions:
In a 4-quart pot, in olive oil, sauté the onion, garlic, and mushrooms over medium heat for 15 minutes until tender. As they cook, add the basil and soy sauce. (Yes, this is an Italian sauce, but that little dash of soy sauce gives the mushrooms a nice lift.) After ten minutes add the tomato sauce and diced tomatoes. Simmer over low heat for one hour. Add the salt, sugar, and cheese. Stir into sauce. Serve over your favorite pasta in a bowl. This sauce keeps well while the flavor improves.
Serves 4-6.

73

Tomato Artichoke Pasta

Ingredients:
1 tb. olive oil
1 tb. fresh crushed garlic
1 medium onion, diced
1 sweet green pepper, diced
2 cups sliced mushrooms
14-oz. can artichoke hearts, quartered
and drained
28-oz. can tomato sauce
14-oz. can diced tomatoes
1 tb. Dijon mustard
juice of one lemon
salt and black pepper to taste
Tabasco sauce to taste
fresh grated Parmesan cheese
1 lb. pasta

Instructions:
In a 4-quart pot, in olive oil, sauté the garlic, onion, green pepper, and sliced mushrooms over medium heat for 15 minutes until tender. Add the artichokes, tomato sauce, diced tomatoes, mustard, lemon, salt, pepper, and Tabasco sauce. Simmer for one hour. Pour the sauce over pasta in a pasta bowl. Sprinkle with freshly grated Parmesan cheese.

Serves 4-6.

Prosciutto, Peas, & Parmesan Pasta

Ingredients:
1 tb. olive oil
1 medium onion, diced
1 tb. fresh crushed garlic
2 cups sliced mushrooms
1/2 gallon whole milk
1/2 cup roux (page 2)
1 lb. sliced strips Prosciutto or
diced ham
1/2 cup freshly grated Asiago or
Parmesan cheese
1 lb. pasta

Instructions:
In a 4-quart pot, in olive oil, sauté the onion, garlic, and mushrooms over medium heat for 15 minutes until tender. Add the milk and simmer to hot (180 degrees) but do not boil. Add the roux and stir until the mixture thickens. Add the Prosciutto or ham. Simmer 10 minutes over low heat. Add the cheese and simmer an additional 5 minutes. If the sauce is too thick for your taste, thin it with up to one cup of dry white wine. Serve over your favorite pasta.

Serves 4-6.

Entrées

The Blue Plate diner has relatively few entrées on its menu. Here are some of the favorites of customers. You can complement these entrées with your favorite potato, rice, or pasta dishes, and with the vegetable or salad of your choice. Here are the stars of the meal, around which the side dishes revolve.

Meatloaf of the Gods

Ingredients:

1 tb. olive oil
1 carrot, diced
2 stalks celery, diced
1/2 sweet green pepper, diced
1 medium onion, diced
1 tb. crushed garlic
1 tb. salt
2 tsp. black pepper
1 tsp. white pepper
1/2 tsp. cayenne
1 tsp. cumin
1/2 tsp. nutmeg
2 lbs. lean ground beef
6 oz. pork sausage
4 eggs
1 cup ketchup
1 cup half-and-half
1 1/2 cups oatmeal

Instructions:

In a 4-quart pan, in olive oil, sauté the carrots, celery, green pepper, onion, and garlic over medium heat for 10 minutes until tender. Add all the seasonings and mix into the vegetables. Add the ground beef and sausage and mix all together. Transfer to a large bowl. Add the eggs, ketchup, half-and-half, and oats. Mix all very thoroughly until it is well blended and smooth. Place into two bread pans and cover them with tinfoil. Bake at 400 degrees for 60 to 90 minutes. Remove the tinfoil and bake for another 10 minutes until the top browns. Drain off excess liquid.

Serves 8 with leftovers for sandwiches the next day.

Zucchini Potato Pancakes

Ingredients:
4 medium zucchinis
2 large baking potatoes
1 medium onion, diced
3 eggs
1/2 cup flour
1 tsp. salt
1 tsp. black pepper
3 tbs. vegetable oil
8 oz. sour cream
8 oz. apple sauce

Instructions:
In a food processor or with a hand grater, grate the zucchinis and potatoes. Mix these with the diced onion in a bowl. Make small handfuls and squeeze out the excess moisture. You may be surprised at how much water is squeezed out. In a separate bowl, combine the vegetables with the eggs, flour, salt, and pepper. Mix thoroughly. Scoop 2- to 3-oz. portions of the pancake mix and flatten with a spatula. In a large non-stick flying pan heated with the vegetable oil, fry over low to medium heat for 10 minutes. When one side is browned, flip the pancake and fry the other side. The edges should be golden crisp. Serve immediately with sour cream and apple sauce.

Serves 4.

Vegetable Curry

Ingredients:

2 large baking potatoes, peeled
and cubed
2 tbs. olive oil
1 head cauliflower, in florets
2 carrots, peeled and sliced
1 stalk celery, sliced
1 medium onion, diced
1 sweet red pepper, diced
1/2 cup raisins
1 cup defrosted green peas
1/2 cup sliced apples
1-2 tbs. curry powder
1/2 tsp. cayenne pepper
2 tbs. honey
1 cup rice, cooked (to yield 3 cups)

Instructions:

Boil the cubed potatoes until tender. Drain, cool, cover, and set aside. In a 4-quart pot, in olive oil, sauté the cauliflower, carrots, celery, onions, and red pepper for 15 minutes until tender. Add the raisins, cooked potatoes, peas, and apples. Mix them together. Add the curry powder, cayenne, and honey and toss. Serve over rice.

Serves 4-6.

Samosas

Ingredients:

Vegetable curry (previous recipe)

Ingredients for pie dough:

4 cups flour
12 oz. margarine
1 tsp. salt
1 tb. sugar
1 1/2 cups cold water

Instructions for pie dough:

Combine the flour, margarine, salt, and sugar in a large mixing bowl. Using two knives or a pastry cutter, chop the margarine into small pieces and slowly add the water until there is a dry dough. You must refrigerate the dough overnight. Make the samosas (pies) the following day. You can take a short cut by buying pie sheets in the refrigerated section of your grocery store.

Instructions for making the samosas:

Using the vegetable curry for filling, roll the pie dough to 1/4-inch thick. Cut the dough into 4-inch circles. Place a heaping tablespoon of the curry filling in the center of each circle. Fold in half, sealing the dough with a fork. (Optional: egg wash each samosa.) Bake on a greased cookie sheet at 375 degrees for 20 to 30 minutes until brown.

Serves 4-6.

Vegetarian Chili

Ingredients:
2 tbs. olive oil
2 stalks celery, diced
1 medium onion, diced
1 green pepper, diced
2 medium carrots, peeled and diced
1 medium zucchini, diced
1 cup sliced mushrooms
1 cup sliced black olives
1 jalapeno pepper, finely diced
1 tb. chili powder
1 tb. cumin
1 tsp. salt
1 tb. black pepper
1/2-tsp. cayenne
6 dashes Tabasco sauce
juice from one lemon
28-oz. can tomato sauce
28-oz. can diced tomatoes
14-oz. can kidney beans, drained
and rinsed
14-oz. can great northern beans,
drained and rinsed

14-oz. can garbanzo beans, drained
and rinsed
2 cups water

Instructions:
In a 6-quart pot, in the olive oil, sauté the celery, onion, green pepper, carrot, zucchini, mushrooms, black olives, and jalapeno pepper over medium heat for 10 minutes until tender. Add all the seasoning and spices and continue to sauté for 5 minutes more. Add the tomato sauce, diced tomatoes, and all the beans. Simmer for one hour on low heat. Add water as needed if the chili becomes too thick. Adjust the seasonings and cayenne to your taste as the chili cooks. Serve with corn bread (next recipe).
Serves 8.

Corn Bread

Ingredients:

2 1/2 cups flour
1 1/2 cups corn meal
1/2 cup sugar
4 tsp. baking powder
1 tsp. salt
4 large eggs
2 cups milk
1/2 cup vegetable oil
1 cup (mixed) diced green and
red sweet peppers
1 cup corn, defrosted

Instructions:

In a large bowl, combine the flour, corn meal, sugar, baking powder, and salt. In a separate bowl, whip the eggs vigorously, then combine them with the milk and oil and stir all together. To the wet mixture add the peppers and corn and stir. Gently blend the wet and dry ingredients. Be careful not to overmix. Pour the mixture into a 9 x 12-inch greased pan. Cover with tinfoil and bake for one hour at 375 degrees. Remove the foil and bake an additional 15-20 minutes until the corn bread is brown and firm.

Serves 8.

Cajun Cordon Bleu

Ingredients:

1 tb. olive oil
1 medium onion, sliced thin
1 sweet green pepper, sliced thin
juice of one lemon
5 dashes Tabasco sauce
1/2 tsp. cayenne
4 boneless/skinless chicken breasts
4 1-oz. slices Provolone cheese
2 eggs
2 cups bread crumbs
1 tb. water

Instructions:

Sauté, in olive oil, the onion and green pepper for 10 minutes until tender. Add the lemon juice, Tabasco, and cayenne pepper. Stir and set aside. Cover each chicken breast in plastic wrap (to avoid splashing) and pound until about 1/4-inch thick. Place in each flattened breast a fourth of the pepper mixture and a slice of the cheese. Roll each breast around its filling. Use a toothpick to hold together. In a small bowl, beat the eggs and water to form an egg wash. Place the bread crumbs into another bowl. Using both hands, dip each chicken roll into the egg wash and dredge in the bread crumbs. Place in a pan and bake at 400 degrees for 20 minutes.

Serves 4.

Chicken Richelieu

Ingredients:

6 boneless/skinless chicken breasts
1 medium onion, diced
1 cup diced mushrooms
1 cup finely-chopped walnuts
1 cup finely-diced ham
1 tb. olive oil
1/2 cup grated Parmesan cheese
1 shot brandy
2 large eggs
1 tb. water
2 cups bread crumbs

Instructions:

Cover each chicken breast in plastic wrap (to avoid splashing) and pound until about 1/4-inch thick. Set aside. In a large frying pan, sauté, in olive oil, the the onion, mushrooms, walnuts, and ham over medium heat for 15 minutes. Add the brandy and mix. While hot, transfer the sautéed mixture into a large bowl. Add the cheese and mix until the cheese melts. This will be the filling for the chicken breasts. Scoop the filling onto the flattened chicken breasts. Roll the breast and use a toothpick to hold it together. In a small bowl, beat the eggs and water to form an egg wash. Place the bread crumbs in another bowl. Using both hands, dip each chicken roll into the egg wash and dredge in the bread crumbs. Place in a pan and bake at 400 degrees for 20 minutes.

Serves 6.

Aztec Chicken

Ingredients:

4 boneless/skinless chicken breasts
1 tb. olive oil
1/2 sweet green pepper, sliced thin
1/2 sweet red pepper, sliced thin
1 medium onion, sliced thin
2 tbs. cumin
2 tbs. chili powder
4 1-oz. slices Provolone or Swiss cheese
4 10-inch flour tortillas

Instructions:

Cover each chicken breast in plastic wrap (to avoid splashing) and pound until about 1/4-inch thick. In a frying pan, in olive oil, sauté the peppers and onion over medium heat for 10 minutes. Dust the peppers and onions with the cumin and chili powder. Place the vegetable mixture evenly on top of the flattened chicken breasts. Top each with one slice of cheese. Roll up the chicken breasts. Place the rolled chicken breast in the center of the tortilla and roll it up, tucking in both ends, burrito-style. Wrap each in tinfoil. Bake at 400 degrees for 20-30 minutes.

Serves 4.

Greek Spinach Pie

Ingredients:

2 tbs. olive oil
2 cups sliced mushrooms
1 medium diced onion
1 tb. crushed garlic
1 cup sliced black olives
4 10-oz. packages defrosted and
    drained spinach
juice from 2 lemons
1 tb. dry oregano
2 cups crumbled Feta cheese
4 tbs. melted butter or margarine
1 package frozen phyllo dough
salt and black pepper to taste

Instructions:

In a 4-quart pot, in olive oil, sauté the mushrooms and onion for 5 minutes over medium heat. Add the garlic and sauté for an additional 15 minutes. Add the olives, spinach, lemon juice, oregano, salt, and pepper. Continue to sauté while stirring 5 more minutes. Remove from the heat, crumble in the Feta cheese, and set aside. Grease a 9 x 12-inch pan and line the bottom with 6 sheets of phyllo dough. Brush the top sheet with melted butter or margarine. Bake this layer in the oven for 10-15 minutes at 400 degrees until golden brown. Remove from the oven and spread spinach mixture over the baked phyllo dough and top with 6 more phyllo sheets. Brush with butter or margarine. Bake 20 minutes at 400 degrees until golden brown.

Serves 6-8.

German Pork

1 cup white wine
1 cup beer
2 tbs. Worcestershire sauce
2 tbs. olive oil

Other ingredients:
2 lbs. boneless pork loin
1/4 lb. bacon, diced
1 medium onion, diced
28-oz. can Bavarian sauerkraut
2 tbs. Dijon or stone-ground mustard
1/2 cup brown sugar
1 qt. mashed potatoes

Instructions:
Mix together all the marinade ingredients with a whisk. Slice the pork loin into thin slices and marinate overnight. When ready to prepare the meal, peel the potatoes and start them boiling. In a frying pan, sauté the bacon over medium heat until the fat is fried out. Drain the grease. Add the onion and continue to sauté for 10 minutes. Add the sauerkraut. Stir in the mustard and brown sugar. Heat for 10 minutes until hot. As it is heating, drain and mash the potatoes and cover. Fry the pork slices for just a few minutes on each side. (They cook quickly and excess cooking will make them tough.) On a 9-inch dinner plate serve generous portions of mashed potatoes and the Bavarian sauerkraut. The fried pork should be served on top of the sauerkraut.

Serves 6-8.

Pineapple Turkey

Ingredients:

1 fresh pineapple, cubed, or 2 14-oz.
cans pineapple, drained (save liquid)

2 tb. soy sauce

1/4 cup cold water

1 tb. corn starch

1 lb. turkey breast, cooked and cubed

6 scallions. sliced

1 small sweet green pepper, diced

1 small sweet red pepper, diced

3/4 cup rice, cooked (to yield 2 cups)

Instructions:

Put the pineapple juice and soy sauce into a sauce pan and bring to a boil. Reserve pineapple chunks. Mix water and corn starch thoroughly. Slowly add to the boiling mixture until it thickens. Set aside to cool at room temperature. Place cubed turkey, scallions, and peppers into a large bowl. Add the pineapple chunks. Stir in the cooked sauce and toss in the rice. Chill. This dish may be served cold, or reheated.

Serves 4-6.

Cod Cakes

Ingredients:

2 lbs. frozen cod
salt and black pepper to taste
Tabasco sauce to taste
2 tbs. olive oil
1 medium onion, diced
3 stalks celery, sliced thin
1 tb. crushed garlic
2 cups sliced mushrooms
1 tb. soy or Worcestershire sauce
3 eggs
1 cup bread crumbs
1 tb. Dijon mustard
1/4 cup grated Parmesan cheese

Instructions:

Defrost cod, place in a pan, and bake in oven at 350 degrees for 20-30 minutes. Remove from the oven and set aside to cool. When cooled, place in a large mixing bowl. Crumble the cod. Add and stir in the salt, pepper, and Tabasco sauce. In a frying pan, in olive oil, sauté the onion, celery, garlic, and mushrooms over medium heat for 10-15 minutes until tender. Add the soy or Worcestershire sauce and continue cooking for 5 additional minutes. Add the sauteed vegetables, eggs, bread crumbs, mustard, and grated cheese to the cod in the mixing bowl. Mix well. Form round 3-inch patties. Place on a greased cookie sheet and bake for 20 minutes at 400 degrees or until firm.

Makes 10 patties.

White Pizza

Ingredients:

1 12-inch home-baked pizza crust (or
store-bought crust)

Ingredients for the pizza crust:

1/4 cup corn meal
4 cups flour
1 tsp. salt
1 tb. sugar
1 tb. oil
1 oz. yeast
2 cups water

Ingredients for the white sauce:

4 cups milk
1/4 cup roux (page 2)
2 cups grated Asiago cheese
white pepper to taste
Tabasco sauce to taste
white wine as needed to thin

Pizza ingredients:

2 tbs. olive oil
1 lb. fresh spinach

2 cups sliced mushrooms
1 medium onion, diced
3 medium tomatoes, sliced

Instructions:

There are four steps to this recipe.

First, to make the crust, mix the corn meal, flour, salt, sugar, oil, yeast, and water in a mixing bowl to form a stiff dough. Cover the bowl and let rise for one hour. (It should approximately double in size.) Punch down the dough and knead into a ball. Set aside for 15 minutes at room temperature. On a floured surface roll the dough ball into a 12-inch flat, round crust. Bake in oven at 400 degrees for 10 minutes. Remove and cool.

To make the white cheese sauce, heat the milk over low flame just until it boils. (Be careful not to scorch the milk.) Add the roux and stir until it dissolves into and thickens the milk. Stir in the Asiago cheese, white pepper, and

Tabasco sauce. Thin the mixture as needed with white wine. Set aside.

To make the topping, sauté, in olive oil, the spinach, mushrooms, and onion over medium heat for 10 minutes until the vegetables are tender.

To construct the pizza, spread the tomato slices over the entire crust. Sprinkle the sauteed vegetables over the tomatoes. Drizzle the white sauce evenly over the top. Bake 15-20 minutes at 400 degrees.

Serves 2-4.

Shepherd's Pie

Ingredients:

3 large baking potatoes
2 tbs. olive oil
1 tb. crushed garlic
1 medium onion, diced
3 stalks celery, diced
2 carrots, sliced thin
1 lb. ground beef
14-oz. can tomato sauce
1 tb. beef base
Tabasco sauce to taste
salt and black pepper to taste

Instructions:

Peel potatoes, cover with water in a 6-quart pot, and boil until tender. While they are cooking, in a large frying pan, in olive oil, sauté the garlic, onion, celery, and carrots over medium heat for 20-30 minutes until the carrots begin to soften. In another pan, brown the ground beef and strain off any excess fat. Add the ground beef to the sauteed vegetables. Add the tomato sauce. Season with the beef base, Tabasco sauce, salt, and pepper. Spread the meat mixture into a pan. Drain and mash the potatoes and spread them evenly over the meat mixture. Bake uncovered at 400 degrees for 20-30 minutes. Remove from the oven and cool for 15 minutes. Cut into squares.

Serves 6.

Mexican Lasagne

Ingredients:
2 tbs. olive oil
2 carrots, sliced thin
3 stalks celery, diced
1 tb. crushed garlic
1 medium onion, diced
14-oz. can whole corn, drained
14-oz. can black beans, drained
14-oz. can diced tomatoes
2 jalapeno peppers (or more),
    finely diced
1/2 tsp. cayenne pepper (or more)
2 tbs. cumin
1 tb. chili powder
12 6-inch flour tortillas
2 cups shredded Cheddar cheese

Instructions:
In a large frying pan, in olive oil, sauté the carrots, celery, garlic, and onion for 10 minutes over medium heat until tender. Add the vegetables and all seasonings. Stir and cook on low heat for 30 minutes. While the vegetables are cooking, line a greased 11 x 7 x 1.5-inch Pyrex dish with a single layer of tortillas, each cut in half. Cover with a layer of the vegetable filling, then a layer of cheese. Continue making such layers—tortillas, vegetables, and cheese—until the dish is filled or the ingredients all used up. Top with shredded cheese. Bake for 30 minutes at 375 degrees.

Serves 6-8.

Kids & Desserts

Kids & Desserts

Kids are not the easiest of people to please with food, as every parent knows. The following menu items are kid-friendly and fun, and they involve the kids in the making as well as the eating. These easy-to-fix recipes are also ideal for children's parties, when the whole group can get involved.

Pizza Pal

Ingredients:
4 English muffins, divided in half
16-oz. jar pizza sauce
2 oz. shredded Mozzarella cheese
1 tb. sliced black olives
strips of green pepper, onion, pimiento,
or other vegetable

Instructions:
Toast the English muffins. Spread with pizza sauce. Top with small amount of Mozzarella cheese. Have the children create funny faces, using the olives and strips of vegetables. Bake Pizza Pals for 5 minutes to melt the cheese.
Serves 4.

KEEP SMILING

Mr. Chippy

Ingredients:
3 large eggs
1 qt. buttermilk
1 tsp. vanilla
2 oz. melted margarine
3 cups flour
1 tsp. salt
3 tbs. sugar
1 tsp. baking soda
1 tsp. baking powder
1/2 cup oats
1 tb. butter
2 oz. miniature chocolate chips

Instructions:
Mix the eggs, buttermilk, vanilla, and margarine until well blended. Separately, stir together the flour, salt, sugar, baking soda, baking powder, and oats. Combine the dry and wet ingredients until they form a smooth batter. In a heated and buttered non-stick pan make 3-inch pancakes. Brown on both sides. Let the kids decorate the pancakes with the chocolate chips.

Serves 4.

Dino Bites

You'll need a dinosaur-shaped cookie cutter for this one.

Ingredients:
4 slices white bread
4 1-oz. slices Cheddar cheese
2 tbs. softened butter

Instructions:
Lightly butter one side of each slice of bread with butter. Place one slice of cheese between two slices of bread with the buttered sides on the outside. In a non-stick frying pan, fry the sandwiches until golden brown on one side, then the other. When the sandwiches are finished, let the children, using the cookie cutter, punch a dinosaur out of the center of the cheese sandwich. Serve with potato chips and a pickle. Save the outside of the cuttings, because the kids will eat them just as readily as the dinosaur. (Of course you may use any other cookie cutters you have in the kitchen.)
Serves 4.

Skabetti

Try to make this kids' dish when you have marinara sauce left over from the previous night's dinner.

Ingredients:
1/2 lb. alphabet noodles
2 cups marinara sauce (see page 72)
4 tbs. grated Parmesan cheese

Instructions:
Cook alphabet noodles. Mix with marinara sauce. Top with Parmesan cheese. Let kids pick out noodles to spell their names. That way you can feed the kids and give them a spelling lesson, too.
Serves 4.

Cup-O-Mud

Ingredients:
1 package Jell-O chocolate
instant pudding
4 Oreo cookies
aerosol can of whipped cream

Instructions:
Follow the instructions on the package for making the instant pudding. Lightly pulverize the Oreo cookies in a food processor or blender. Combine with the chocolate pudding. Let kids squirt on the whipped cream from the aerosol can.
Serves 4.

Fish Tank

Nine-ounce clear plastic glasses work well for this recipe.

Ingredients:
3 oz. package "Berry Blue" Jell-O
2 dozen gummy fish

Instructions:
Follow the package directions to make the Jello. Pour into the glasses and cool. Just as the Jello begins to set, add the gummy fish to each glass and stir them into the Jello. Continue to cool the Jello until it is firm. Let the kids marvel at the fish in the "tank."

Serves 4.

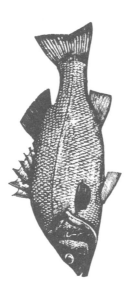 

Desserts

The Blue Plate Diner serves a broad array of home-style baked pies, cookies, muffins, scones, and cakes. Portions tend to be generous and these treats are natural, made without preservatives. (Blue Plate desserts don't stay around long enough to need preservatives.) Just as many desserts are carried out the door as are consumed in the diner.

Sara Whalen, the bakery chef, has been baking professionally for twelve years. After having been a homemaker and child care provider for many years, she answered a newspaper ad that asked, "Do you like to bake? We will train you to bake for our restaurant, the Ovens of Brittany."

That sounded like a good change of pace for Sara, and she has been baking for others ever since. Sara was the oldest of six children, so she had the opportunity to start baking at an early age. Her brothers teased her, claiming that her cookies were not as good as their mother's, but they didn't turn down the cookies, either. When Sara's own children were young, she learned to make bread, and for many years provided all the family's bread. The best testers of Sara's recipes are her husband, John, and their children Anne, John, Nora, and Ruth.

Here are some of Sara's favorite recipes—which are, not surprisingly, some favored by Blue Plate diners as well.

Apple Pie

Apple pie in its several variations is the most popular fruit pie. The Blue Plate Diner uses frozen apple slices, but you may use fresh apples of the season. This recipe fills a deep 9 1/2-inch glass pie plate.

Ingredients:
8 cups sliced apples
3/4 to 1 cup sugar (depending on tartness of apples)
1/3 cup flour
2 tsp. cinnamon
1/4 tsp. nutmeg
1 tb. lemon juice
1 prepared double pie crust, or 2 homemade crusts

Instructions:
Peel and slice apples into a bowl. Add the remaining ingredients except the crusts and toss with apples. Put into a crust-lined pie place and top with the second crust. Cut off excess and pinch the crusts around the edges to seal apple mixture. Bake at 350 degrees for one hour, until the apples are bubbly and crust is nice and brown.

Caramel Apple Pie with Streusel Topping

You may make a different version of the standard apple pie by adding walnuts and caramel to the recipe. This version uses no top crust. To the recipe on page 103 add the following ingredients:

6 caramels
1/4 cup chopped walnuts
1/2 tsp. cinnamon

Streusel ingredients:
2 tbs. butter
1/3-cup sugar
1/3 cup flour
1/2 tsp. cinnamon

Instructions:
Put half the apples into the crust-lined pie plate. Soften the caramels and spread over the apples. Spread the walnuts across the top of the apples. Sprinkle the remaining 1/2 tsp. of cinnamon on the apples and walnuts. Cover with the remaining apple mixture. To make the streusel, blend together the softened butter, sugar, flour, and cinnamon. After it is blended, sprinkle over the pie. Bake for one hour until the streusel is browned and the apple filling is bubbling.

Cranberry-Apple Pie

Cranberry-apple pie is another popular version of the basic apple pie recipe. Simply decrease the apples by one cup and add one cup of chopped cranberries. Cover with the second crust, then cut and pinch the edges. Or use streusel topping instead of a top crust. Bake at 350 degrees for one hour.

Spinach & Cheese Scones

Ingredients:

3 cups flour
1 tb. baking powder
1/3 tsp. salt
1 tb. dried basil
1 tb. dried oregano
2/3 tsp. cayenne pepper
2/3 tsp. garlic powder
1 tsp. dried parsley
1/4 lb. butter
1/4 cup thawed spinach, squeezed dry
1/2 cup shredded Cheddar cheese
1/2 cup grated Parmesan cheese
3/4 cup milk
3 eggs
1 egg white (as wash)

Instructions:

In a large mixing bowl, blend together all the dry ingredients. Cut in the butter until the mixture is like cornmeal. Blend in the spinach and the cheeses. In a separate bowl, combine and whip together the milk and eggs. Stir the egg mixture into the flour mixture until well combined. Turn the combined mixture onto a floured surface and knead gently. When the mixture is combined, roll it to 3/4-inch to one inch thick. Do not overwork. Cut into 3-inch rounds with a biscuit cutter. Place on a greased baking sheet and brush with the egg white for a shiny finish. Bake in the oven at 350 degrees for 20 minutes.

Yield 8 scones.

Sugar Cookies

Cut-out cookies have become a daily item at the Blue Plate Diner. The bakers have a collection of cookie cutters and enjoy making some unique cookies. Children especially like dinosaur and Big Foot cookies. They eat the toes first!

Ingredients:
1/2 lb. butter
2 cups sugar
2 eggs
2 tsp. vanilla
3 1/2 cups flour
2 tsp. baking powder
2 tsp. salt

Instructions:
Cream softened butter and sugar until light and fluffy. Add eggs and vanilla. Mix until well blended. In a separate bowl mix the dry ingredients. Add to the creamed mixture. Mix until the flour is blended into the cream mixture. Chill for 2 hours or more. Roll the dough to 1/4-inch thick. Use any cookie cutter. Bake at 350 degrees for 8-10 minutes. Remove from oven and cool. Spread with frosting.

Cookie Frosting
Ingredients:
1 lb. powdered sugar
2 oz. water
1 tb. powdered sugar
2 oz. water
1 tb. corn syrup
pinch of cream of tarter
1 tsp. vanilla
1 tb. butter

Instructions:
Put powdered sugar in a mixing bowl with cream of tarter. Heat water, butter, and corn syrup in the microwave until butter melts. Add to sugar and beat until smooth. Mix in vanilla. This frosting spreads nicely on the cookies while it is still warm. If frosting becomes too stiff to spread easily, warm in the microwave. Tint frosting with food colors of your choice.

Coconut Cream Pie

This pie is made in three stages. There will be ingredients and instructions for each stage.

Stage 1. Ingredients
prepared pie crust (or your
home-made crust)
4 cups whole milk
1/2 cup sugar

Instructions:
Place the pie crust into a deep 9 1/2-inch pie pan and bake at 350 degrees until golden. Remove from oven and set aside. Mix the milk and sugar in a large microwave-safe bowl. Microwave on high until the milk is very hot, almost boiling. Set aside.

Stage 2. Ingredients:
1/2 cup sugar
1/2 cup cornstarch
dash salt
2 large eggs
4 egg yolks

Instructions:
In another bowl, whisk together the sugar, cornstarch, salt, eggs, and egg yolks. Gradually add the egg mixture to the hot milk mixture. Cook for one minute on high in the microwave. Stop and stir. Continue this procedure until the mixture thickens. Set aside.

Stage 3. Ingredients:
2 oz. butter
1 1/2 tsp. vanilla
3 cups shredded coconut
toasted coconut for garnish

Instructions:
Add the butter, vanilla, and all but 1/4 cup of coconut to the thickened mixture. Toast remaining 1/4 cup of coconut in the oven until light brown. (You can do this while the crust is baking.) Pour thickened mixture into the baked pie crust. Sprinkle with the toasted coconut. Cool and refrigerate.

Chocolate & Banana Cream Pie

The recipe for coconut cream pie is wonderfully versatile. If you want to make a chocolate pie, omit the coconut and add 3 cups of chocolate chips in the last step. Stir until the chips are melted and blended. To make a banana cream pie, omit the coconut and add slices from 2 large, ripe bananas. Space the banana slices between layers of the vanilla pudding in the pie shell.

Pumpkin Muffins

Ingredients:

1 1/2 cup sugar
1/2 cup oil
2 eggs
1 cup canned pumpkin puree
1 1/2 tsp. vanilla
1/4 cup water
1 3/4 cups flour
1 1/2 tsp. baking soda
3/4 tsp. salt
3/4 tsp. cinnamon
1/2 tsp. nutmeg
1/2 tsp. allspice
1/4 tsp. powdered ginger
pinch ground cloves

Instructions:

Preheat oven to 350 degrees. Oil a standard-size muffin tin. Set aside. In a large mixing bowl, beat together the sugar, oil, and eggs. Add the pumpkin, vanilla, and water. Mix well. Combine all dry ingredients with the wet and stir until just blended. The batter should be completely smooth. Fill each muffin tin 3/4 full. Bake for 25-30 minutes.

Makes 12 muffins.

Cheesecakes

Using a basic recipe, the Blue Plate Diner creates a variety of cheesecakes to suit every taste. Once you have mastered the basic recipe, you, too, can exercise your imagination, using chocolate, nuts, and other flavorings, in creating great cheesecakes.

Crust ingredients:
1 cup flour
1/4 cup sugar
1/4 cup softened butter

Instructions for crust:
In a bowl, combine the flour and sugar. With a pastry cutter or two forks, cut butter into the mix until it forms pea-sized crumbs. Pat the mixture into a 10-inch springform pan. Bake at 350 degrees for 10 minutes or until browned.

Filling ingredients:
2 1/2 lbs. cream cheese at room temperature
1 cup sugar
2 tbs. flour
6 eggs
2 1/2 tsp. vanilla
1/2 cup heavy cream

Instructions for the filling:
Cream the cheese with an electric mixer, scraping the bowl with a spatula several times. When the cheese is softened, add the sugar, flour, eggs, and vanilla and beat until the mixture is smooth. Add cream and again mix until smooth. Add the eggs and continue mixing and scraping the bowl sides until thoroughly combined. Pour the filling mixture into the springform pan. Bake for one hour at 300 degrees and until the middle doesn't jiggle when nudged. Turn off the oven and remove the cheesecake when the oven has cooled (about 1/2 hour). Loosen the sides of the cheesecake with a small knife or spatula. Remove the cake from the pan when cooled.

Variations:

To make any of these variations, follow the basic cheesecake recipe, then blend the special ingredients into the prepared filling and pour over the baked crust.

Chocolate Mint Cheesecake

5 tbs. creme de menthe
1 tbs. peppermint extract
1 cup chocolate chips

Candy Bar Cheesecake

1 cup chopped Snickers or toffee bar

Oreo Cheesecake

1 cup chopped Oreo cookies

Joyful Almond Cheesecake

1 cup mini-chocolate chips
1 cup coconut
1 cup toasted sliced almonds

Glaze for Cheesecakes

Ingredients:

1/4 cup heavy cream
1 tb. sugar
1 tb. butter
3/4 cup chocolate chips
1 tb. strong hot coffee

Instructions:

Combine the cream, sugar, and butter in a microwave-safe container and heat until boiling. Add the chocolate chips and whisk until the glaze is shiny and smooth. Whisk in the hot coffee. The glaze should be spread while warm. You may store it in the refrigerator and reheat it when needed.

About Tim Lloyd

I've got cooking in my genes! My father always cooked in our house. He was a cook on a Merchant Marine ship. His claim to fame was a short stint as the broiler chef at the Grand Hotel on Mackinac Island. My maternal grandmother was one of the best natural gourmets I've ever known, a pinch of this and a handful of that. That's how I cook! I just always had a natural feel.

From an early age I understood that cooking was a labor of love. After high school, I attended the Hotel and Restaurant Cookery class at Milwaukee Area Technical College. School was interrupted by a few years of factory work and the pursuit of a college degree in English literature.

I returned to my true love, cooking, in 1976. I worked as a pastry chef at Latham Smith Lodge in Door County. After I moved to Madison, I made sandwiches at Ella's Deli, then created soups at the Esquire Club. Finally, I mastered entrées and sauces at the Ovens of Brittany.

Each of these experiences was a stepping stone in developing my skills and knowledge as a chef. I have found the experience of cooking to be a far better teacher than the classroom.

—Tim Lloyd

About James Novak

James Novak has undergraduate degrees in both philosophy and business administration along with a graduate degree in theology and psychology. He began his career in the hospitality industry in 1972 as kitchen manager for the Blue Gargoyle Coffee House at the University of Chicago. He was hired by AT&T to manage one of their Chicago "Loop" employee cafeterias after an interview in which he said that "eating is a sacred function where friends and family gather together."

In 1974 he was named director of a five-unit dining service at St. Joseph's College in Rensselaer, Indiana. Later, a thirst to own his own business led him to purchase Red Shed in Madison. After five years, he sold the business and became director of purchasing for the Ovens of Brittany, for which he established an innovative purchasing program.

In 1993, Novak initiated the Buy Right Purchasing Group, which gathers independent restaurants into a buying unit. Buy Right enters into master contracts for these independent restaurants, giving them the purchasing power of larger chain restaurants. Twenty-five independent restaurants in the Madison area now make up the Buy Right Purchasing Group.

Novak's parents were married during the Great Depression. His mother worked while his father sought employment. Novak was inspired to cook while watching his father cater to his mother as she came home from work for meals. He will never forget his father's frequent "hobo" soups.

INDEX

INDEX

INDEX